My Twenty Five Years in Provence

Peter Mayle

Conversation Starters

By Paul Adams
Book Habits

Please Note: This is an unofficial Conversation Starters guide. If you have not yet read the original work, you can purchase the original book here.

Copyright © 2018 by BookHabits. All Rights Reserved. First Published in the United States of America 2018

We hope you enjoy this complementary guide from BookHabits. Our mission is to aid readers and reading groups with quality, thought provoking material to in the discovery and discussions on some of today's favorite books.

Disclaimer / Terms of Use: This guide is unofficial and unauthorized. It is not authorized, approved, licensed, or endorsed by the original book's author or publisher and any of their licensees or affiliates. Product names, logos, brands, and other trademarks featured or referred to within this publication are the property of their respective trademark holders and are not affiliated with BookHabits. The publisher and author make no representations or warranties with respect to the accuracy or completeness of these contents and disclaim all warranties such as warranties of fitness for a particular purpose.
No part of this publication may be reproduced or retransmitted, electronic or mechanical, without the written permission of the publisher.

Bonus Downloads
*Get Free Books with **Any Purchase** of* Conversation Starters!

Every purchase comes with a FREE download!

Add spice to any conversation
Never run out of things to say
Spend time with those you love

Get it Now

or Click Here.

Scan Your Phone

Tips for Using Conversation Starters:

EVERY GOOD BOOK CONTAINS A WORLD FAR DEEPER THAN the surface of its pages. Questions herein are designed to bring us beneath the surface of the page and invite us into the world that lives on. These questions can be used to:

- Foster a deeper understanding of the book
- Promote an atmosphere of discussion for groups
- Assist in the study of the book, either individually or corporately
- Explore unseen realms of the book as never seen before

Table of Contents

Introducing *My Twenty Five Years in Provence* 6
Discussion Questions 13
Introducing the Author 34
Fireside Questions 40
Quiz Questions 51
Quiz Answers 64
Ways to Continue Your Reading 65

Introducing *My Twenty Five Years in Provence*

THE LATE PETER MAYLE IS THE BELOVED author of fifteen books inspired by the charm of Provence. In his last book *My Twenty-Five Years in Provence: Reflections on Then and Now,* he chronicles the lessons he learned, the delights he enjoyed and the changes he observed in the twenty-five years he and his wife spent in the picturesque Provence. Time has passed swiftly since the time Peter and his wife Jennie set off for Aix-en-Provence. Their initial plan was to spend sunny days in Côte d'Azur but the skies were gloomy and the days were rainy. Their detour proved to be one of the best decisions they made. Peter and Jennie fell in love with Provence. They were enchanted by the life there. In no time, they uprooted their lives in England and moved to Provence. Since then, they never looked back. They fell in love with the charm of village life, the ancient history that lives through the metropolitan bustle of Marseilles, the lavender fields that bloom evey sprint and all the magic that Provence has to offer. In his twenty-five years in Provence, he witnessed changes that modern life brought to Provence yet Mayle testifies that the magic remained.

In this one-of-a-kind guide to Provence, Mayle tells of his beautiful memories here. One memory he shared happens on midsummer nights in

Provence. From May to October, every Tuesday, technology gives way to an evening market or *marché nocturne*. Mayle says that to live across the road from Lourmarin is a great advantage. It was one of Luberon's most popular and prettiest villages The tourists and residents who spent the day under the sun could find shade to be relieved from the heat and wine to be relieved from the thirst. The market has a generous array of fresh produce and it introduced professional cuisine to those who came. The fine cuisine are offered by different local chefs who cook there each week. They are assisted by the mayor of the village of Loumarin. He serves as the master of ceremonies and introduces the chef of the week to the people. There are a total of nine chefs who take a break from their busy restaurants to share their expertise in the kitchen. One week the chef of the week would share the secrets of the perfect pasta, that would be made with local olives, cherry tomatoes and olive oil. The next week, anoher chef would feature his signature strawberry dessert. The chef's menu is quite long, varied, simple yet fascinating. And sitting on the wooden benches, the audience are engrossed. Before the turn of the chefs, the night market starts to become busy.

In summer, they hold an informal fashion show that features ladies whose dresses become more transparent each week, their shorts seem to get even shorter, and the design of the hats can make any milliner swoon. The men's dress code varies. In one occasion, the men would sport an aging hippie with silver bracelets, tattoos and a ponytail. On another, the men would sport suits, suede moccasin, and polo shirts that is every bit spotless and iconic Parisian. Whatever the men and women would wear, the crowds would sit and enjoy the show.

Around six o'clock, couples would sit around tin tables. The husbands would lay claim of two chairs while his wife goes shopping around the stalls. She is spoiled with many choices but she would find a couple of horrors too. First there is no trace of bubble wraps, shrink wraps or any kind of plastic packaging. The growers would like you to see what you will eat without any wrappings or trimmings. Another thing absent in the market is the supermarket cart that could be dangerous to the people walking by the market. The only shopping aid on wheels that Mayle saw was the oversized roller skate of a German gentleman.

USA Today's Ashley Day describes *My Twenty-Five Years in Provence,* "endearing . . . Short and sweet." Beth J. Harpaz for *Associated Press* says that this book "treads delightfully familiar ground for fans who succumbed to the charms of Mayle's first book." Maureen McCarthy for *Minneapolis Star-Tribune* says that this book is "[a] well-loved writer's contented recap of a life well lived." Carla Jean Whitley for *BookPage* describes the book "a bittersweet pleasure." *Library Journal* says that Peter Mayle's memoir is for the devoted readers who searches for "confirmation that daydreams do come true." *Publishers Weekly* says that Mayle's final book "is a breezy valedictory note for a much admired writer."

Discussion Questions

"Get Ready to Enter a New World"

Tip: Begin with questions dealing with broader issues to ensure ample time for quality discussions. Read through all discussion questions before engaging.

~~~

question 1

In his final book, Peter Mayle shares how he first arrived in Aix-en-Provence, twenty-five years ago. Who was he with when he first set off to Provence?

~~~

~~~

question 2

A trip to Provence was not his initial plan. He wanted to spend a sunny vacation in one of France's best coastline. What was Mayle's initial destination in France?

~~~

~~~

question 3

In his twenty-five years in Provence, Peter Mayle witnessed changes that modern life brought to Provence. What were the changes that Mayle witnessed through the years?

~~~

~~~

question 4

On midsummer nights in Provence, from May to October, the village holds an evening market. If it wasn't midsummer and there's no night market, what does the village usually offer?

~~~

~~~

question 5

Marché nocturne happens from May to October. The market sells generous food choices for everyone's tastes. What day is the evening market open?

~~~

~~~

question 6

The market has a generous array of fresh produce and it introduced professional cuisine to those who came. The night market is located in one of Luberon's most popular and prettiest villages. What is this village?

~~~

~~~

question 7

The fine cuisine in the night market are offered by different local chefs who cook there each week. They are assisted by the master of ceremonies. Who is this master of ceremonies?

~~~

~~~

question 8

The women who go shopping around the stalls are spoiled with many choices but they would find a couple of horrors too. What are these horrors?

~~~

~~~

question 9

People who shop around the stalls of the night market usually find that there is no trace of bubble wraps, shrink wraps or any kind of plastic packaging. Why is this so?

~~~

~~~

question 10

The local night market also does not have the supermarket carts. The only shopping aid on wheels that Mayle saw was the oversized roller skate of a German gentleman. Why are carts absent in the night market?

~~~

question 11

Walking around the night market on foot would take half an hour. There are cheeses and sausages displayed on trays. What did Mayle notice about the meats, cheeses and other produce in the night market?

~~~

question 12

In the night market, there's a bar. Mayle noticed a young girl, perhaps nine years old who ordered Muscat and was served by the barman. What was Mayle's reaction to this scene?

~~~

question 13

At about seven thirty, the night market begins to look like a bustling café. Most of the market shopping is done, and it's now time for refreshments. What do the French people usually order?

~~~

question 14

In the twenty five years that Peter and his wife Jennie have lived in Provence, they had beautiful adventures. One of which was finding a home. How did Peter and Jennie find their home in Provence?

~~~

question 15

Peter Mayle acknowledged the fact that he indeed was lucky to be living in a sunny place like Provence. According to him, what can you expect from friends if you live in such a lovely place?

~~~

~~~

question 16

Beth J. Harpaz for *Associated Press* says that this book "treads delightfully familiar ground for fans who succumbed to the charms of Mayle's first book." What is the characteristic of Mayle's writing that captured his readers since his first book?

~~~

question 17

Maureen McCarthy for *Minneapolis Star-Tribune* says that this book is "[a] well-loved writer's contented recap of a life well lived." How does the news about his death shed a different light on the words of his final book?

~~~

question 18

Library Journal says that Peter Mayle's memoir is for the devoted readers who searches for "confirmation that daydreams do come true." Why are readers enamored by novels and memoirs set in a dreamy place like Provence?

~~~

~~~

question 19

Publishers Weekly says that Mayle's final book "is a breezy valedictory note for a much admired writer." What do people admire most about the late Peter Mayle? How does is this book a 'valedictory note' for him?

~~~

question 20

San Francisco Chronicle's Regan McMahon praises Mayle's writing that he described him as "astute at capturing the rhythm of life [in Provence]." How did Mayle capture the rhythm of life in Provence? What about the life in this place that captivates Mayle's readers?

~~~

Introducing the Author

THE LATE PETER MAYLE WAS A NOTABLE British author who was famous for his memoirs of his life in Provence, France. Mayle was born in Oxshott in Surrey, England. He was the youngest of the three children. Their family moved to Barbados after World War II. His father was assigned there as an employee of the Colonial Office. Peter Mayle left his school in Barbados at the age of 16. He returned to London. In 1957, he had his first job as a trainee at the London office of *Shell Oil*. It was in this job that Peter Mayle found out that he doesn't like to work with fuel and instead he discovered his interest in advertising. He then wrote to the head of the advertising agency that was hired by Shell during this time. His name was David Ogilvy and Mayle asked him for a job. David Ogilvy responded positively to his letter and offered him a job as a junior account executive. Mayle asked if he can work on the creative side of the business that has been his interest and passion. He subsequently received an offer for another job, this time as a copywriter. In 1961, Mayle worked at the New York office of the advertising agency.

As he was working here, *Papert Koenig*, another advertising agency, poached Mayle from Ogilvy. *Papert Koenig* sent him back to London as the head of the creative team in their office in United

Kingdom. One of Peter Mayle's colleagues was Alan Parker. When the parent company in the United States had trouble during the mid-1960s, Mayle and another colleague purchased the London operations office. They developed the business and got the accounts of big-time companies like *Sony, Watneys* and *Olivetti*. After five years, one of the top American agencies *BBDO* bought their company. Peter Mayle remained in the company as its creative director and he commuted between the UK and the US. In 1972, Mayle wrote the advertising slogan for Wonderloaf Bread. This slogan was used as a slogan by Tottenham Hotspur's supporters and the inspiration of the song *Nice One Cyril*.

In 1974, Mayle quit advertising and pursued a full-time writing career. Mayle moved from Devon to Luberon in the late 1980s. His plans to write a novel was overtaken by his new life in this new environment. This resulted to his international bestselling book *A Year in Provence.* He chronicled his first year as an expatriate in the village of Ménerbes. More books followed and they were translated into more than twenty languages. In 1993, a TV series was produced based on his book *A Year in Provence.* This show starred John Thaw. In 2006, his novel *A Good Year* became the inspiration for Ridley Scott's film of the same name. The characters were played by Russell Crowe and Marion Cotillard. Mayle moved to New York to get away from his fans and other tourists at his home in Provence. He returned to France after a few years. At the time of his death in January 2018, Mayle resided in Vaugines, Luberon, Provence. He died in the hospital near his home.

His book *A Year in Provence* was named Best Travel Book of the Year by British Book Awards in 1989. In 2002, Peter Mayle was made a Knight of the Legion of Honor or *Chevalier de la Légion d'honneur* by the French government for his "*coopération et francophonie.*"

Bonus Downloads
*Get Free Books with **Any Purchase** of Conversation Starters!*

Every purchase comes with a FREE download!

Add spice to any conversation
Never run out of things to say
Spend time with those you love

Get it Now

or Click Here.

Scan Your Phone

Fireside Questions

"What would you do?"

Tip: These questions can be a fun exercise as it spurs creativity among the readers by allowing alternate scene endings and "if this was you" questions.

~~~

question 21

When Peter Mayle was young, their family moved to Barbados after World War II. His father was assigned there as an employee of the Colonial Office. How did this experience as a young man teach Mayle about life overseas?

~~~

question 22

When the parent company in the United States had trouble during the mid-1960s, Mayle and another colleague purchased the London operations office. After five years, one of the top American agencies *BBDO* bought their company. What could be Mayle's reasons for selling his advertising company?

~~~

question 23

In spite of his love for his dear Provence, Peter Mayle moved to New York to get away from his fans and other tourists at his home in Provence. How difficult does it become for writers when fans invade their privacy?

~~~

~~~

question 24

In 2002, Peter Mayle was made a Knight of the Legion of Honor or *Chevalier de la Légion d'honneur* by the French government for his "*coopération et francophonie.*" How did Peter Mayle earn this honor from the French government?

~~~

~~~

question 25

In 2006, Peter Mayle's novel *A Good Year* became the inspiration for Ridley Scott's film of the same name. The characters were played by Russell Crowe and Marion Cotillard. Which of Mayle's other novels can be great subjects for a film?

~~~

~~~

question 26

When Peter and Jennie fell in love with the charm of Provence, they uprooted the lives they built in Devon to move to Provence. If you had the resources, would you also uproot your life and move to Provence?

~~~

question 27

Peter Mayle acknowledged the fact that he indeed was lucky to be living in a sunny place like Provence. According to him, you expect from friends to visit frequently. If you were in Mayle's place, how would you turn away unexpected visitors?

~~~

~~~

question 28

One of the first adventures that Peter and his wife Jennie has was finding a home. If you were Peter and Jennie, which location for a home would you choose? The one near the Côte d'Azur region or in one of the villages in the valley?

~~~

~~~

question 29

Peter and his wife Jennie's initial plan was to spend sunny days in Côte d'Azur but the skies were gloomy and the days were rainy. Their detour led them to Aix-en-Provence. If you were Peter and Jennie, would you also take a detour or will you wait for the skies to clear up in Côte d'Azur?

~~~

~~~

question 30

In the twenty-five years Peter and Jennie spent in Provence, they tried to learned French. If you were an expatriate like they were, would you also learn the language of the place where you live? Or would you stick to your own language since most people understand what you say?

~~~

Quiz Questions

"Ready to Announce the Winners?"

Tip: Create a leaderboard and track scores to see who gets the most correct answers. Winners required. Prizes optional.

~~~

quiz question 1

The fine cuisine in the night market are offered by different local chefs. They are assisted by the master of ceremonies. Who is this master of ceremonies?

~~~

~~~

quiz question 2

Peter Mayle shares how he first arrived in Aix-en-Provence twenty-five years ago. Who was he with when he first set off to Provence?

~~~

~~~

quiz question 3

A trip to Provence was a detour. He wanted to spend a sunny vacation in one of France's best coastline. What was Mayle's initial destination in France?

~~~

~~~

quiz question 4

Marché nocturne happens every week from May to October. What day of the week is the night market open?

~~~

~~~

quiz question 5

True or False: There are a total of twenty chefs who take a break from their busy restaurants to share their expertise in the kitchen. One week the chef of the week would share the secrets of the perfect pasta, then the next week, another chef would feature his signature dessert.

~~~

~~~

quiz question 6

True or False: In the night market, the stalls have generous choices but little to no packaging. There is no trace of bubble wraps, shrink wraps or any kind of plastic packaging.

~~~

~~~

quiz question 7

True or False: Peter and his wife Jennie first set off for Lille when they needed a detour. Their initial plan was to spend sunny days in Marseille but the skies were gloomy and the days were rainy.

~~~

quiz question 8

In 1957, Peter Mayle had his first job as a trainee at the London office of _____. It was in this job that he discovered his interest in advertising. He then wrote to the head of the advertising agency that was hired by his employer during this time.

~~~

quiz question 9

In 1972, Mayle wrote the advertising slogan for Wonderloaf Bread. This slogan was used as a slogan by Tottenham Hotspur's supporters and the inspiration of the song _____.

~~~

~~~

quiz question 10

In 2006, his novel _____ became the inspiration for Ridley Scott's film of the same name. The characters were played by Russell Crowe and Marion Cotillard.

~~~

~~~

quiz question 11

True or False: While Peter Mayle was working with David Ogilvy, another advertising agency poached Mayle from Ogilvy. The company *Papert Koenig* made him the head of the creative team in their office in United Kingdom.

~~~

~~~

quiz question 12

True or False: In 2002, Peter Mayle was made a Knight of the Legion of Honor or *Chevalier de la Légion d'honneur* by the French government for his *"coopération et francophonie."*

~~~

Quiz Answers

1. The Mayor
2. His wife Jennie
3. Côte d'Azur
4. Tuesdays
5. False
6. True
7. False
8. *Shell Oil*
9. *Nice One Cyril*
10. *A Good Year*
11. True
12. True

Ways to Continue Your Reading

EVERY month, our team runs through a wide selection of books to pick the best titles for readers and reading groups, and promotes these titles to our thousands of readers – sometimes with free downloads, sale dates, and additional brochures.

[Click here to sign up for these benefits.](#)

If you have not yet read the original work or would like to read it again, you can purchase the original book here.

Bonus Downloads
*Get Free Books with **Any Purchase** of* Conversation Starters!

Every purchase comes with a FREE download!

Add spice to any conversation
Never run out of things to say
Spend time with those you love

Get it Now

or Click Here.

Scan Your Phone

On the Next Page...

If you found this book helpful to your discussions and rate it a 4 or 5, please write us a review on the next page.

Any length would be fine but we'd appreciate hearing you more! We'd be very encouraged.

Till next time,

BookHabits

"*Loving Books is Actually a Habit*"

CPSIA information can be obtained
at www.ICGtesting.com
Printed in the USA
BVHW03s1120091018
529682BV00002B/240/P